RACHEL PORTMAN ask the river

Edited by James Welland
Additional arrangements by Alistair Watson and Rachel Portman
Still photography by Elspeth Parsons
Manuscripts by Rachel Portman

All the tracks from *ask the river* are on Node Records (www.noderecords.com)
and available to listen to and/or purchase from all major streaming services
worldwide including Spotify, Apple Music and iTunes.

ISBN 978-1-7051-0495-8

Published by

T0057807

Visit Hal Leonard Online at
www.halleonard.com

Contact us:
Hal Leonard
7777 West Bluemound Road
Milwaukee, WI 53213
Email: info@halleonard.com

In Europe, contact:
Hal Leonard Europe Limited
42 Wigmore Street
Marylebone, London, W1U 2RN
Email: info@halleonardeurope.com

In Australia, contact:
Hal Leonard Australia Pty. Ltd.
4 Lentara Court
Cheltenham, Victoria, 3192 Australia
Email: info@halleonard.com.au

I wrote this collection of pieces throughout 2019. They are the fruit of many years spent being immersed in nature. What can be more inspiring than the green shoots of new beech leaves appearing in the woods with the dappling light reflected in the spring breeze?

These pieces are a personal reflection on the beauty of the earth around us – the trees, flora, rivers, birds, animals and all her gifts to us. I hope you enjoy exploring them as much as I loved being inspired by the natural world.

Rachel Portman

LEAVES AND TREES

leaves and trees

Rachel Portman

Gently, evenly, poco rubato ♩ = *c.* 108

leaves and trees

leaves and trees

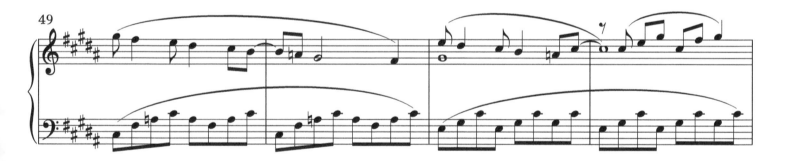

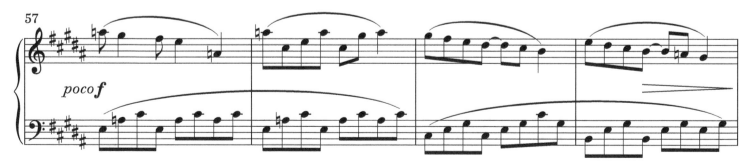

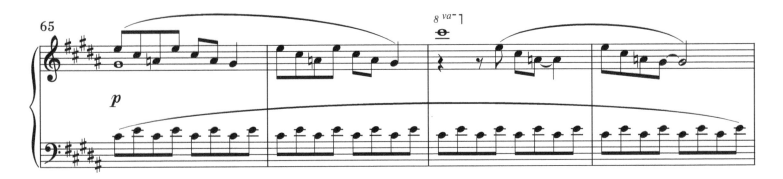

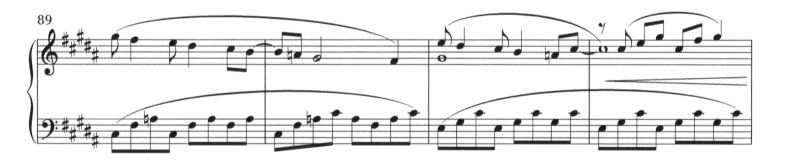

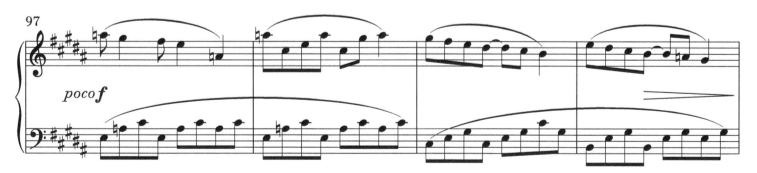

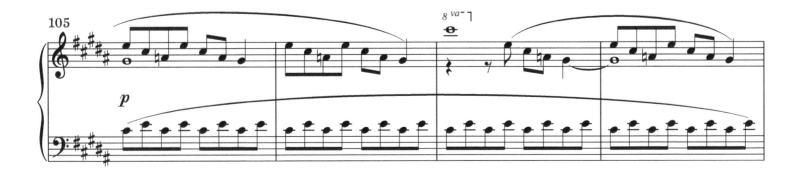

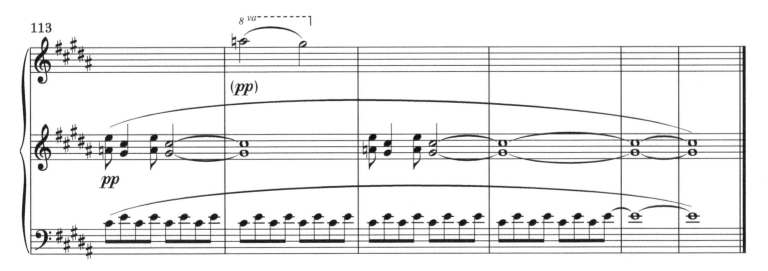

A Gift

a gift

Rachel Portman

a gift

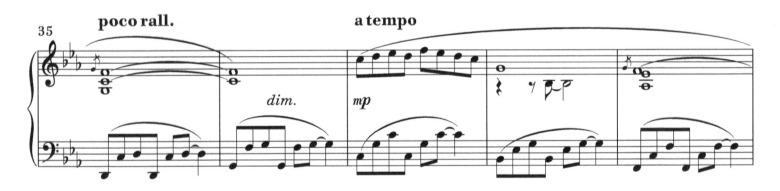

a gift

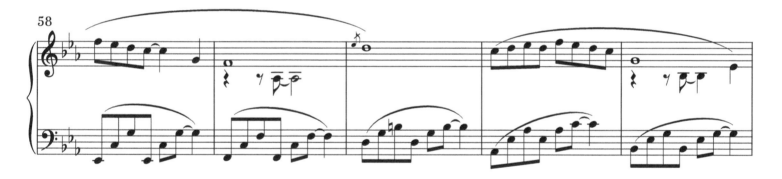

17

Much Loved

much loved

Rachel Portman

Gently, tender; with rubato ♩ = 76

con Ped.

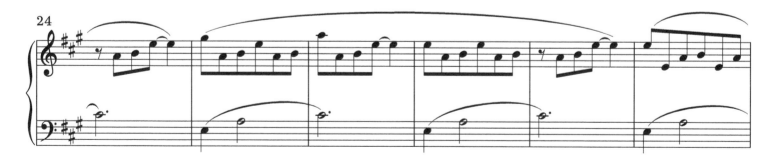

much loved

much loved

rall.

meno mosso

RIVERBED

Rachel Portman 2019

ask the river

RACHEL PORTMAN

Flowing ♩ = c. 104

mp let the dynamics gently ebb and flow

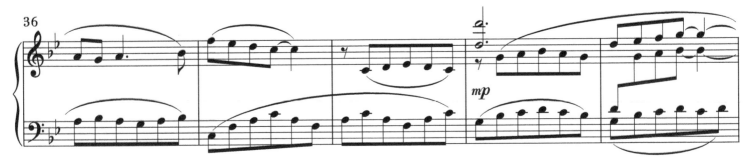

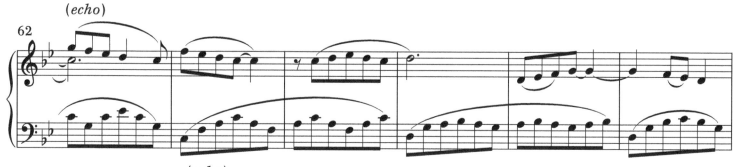

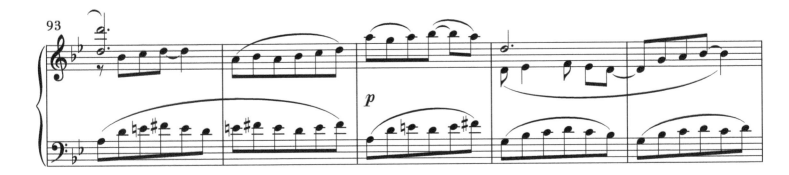

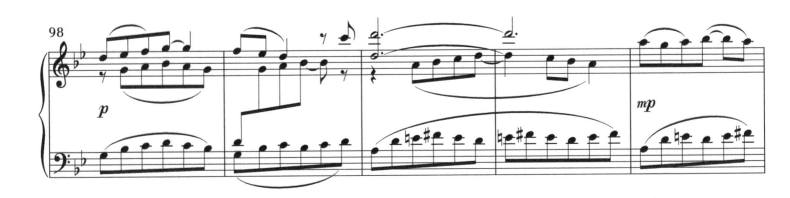

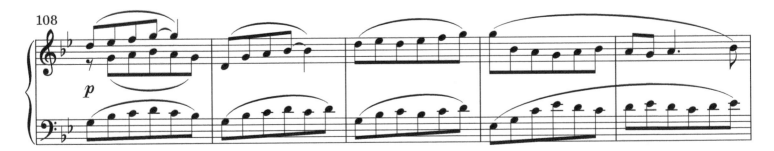

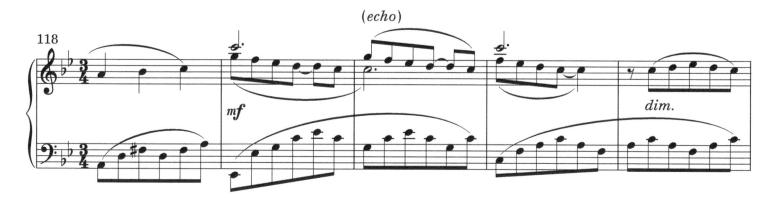

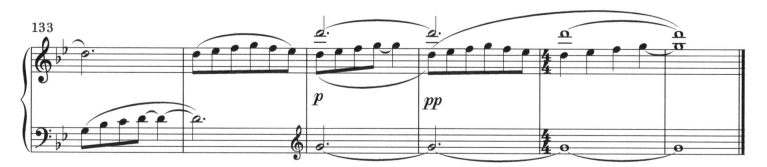

still here

RACHEL PORTMAN

Lightly, poco rubato ♩ = c. 92

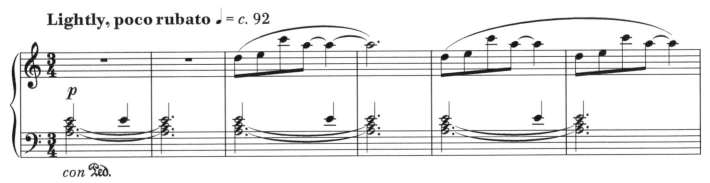

rall.

Poco più mosso ♩ = 108

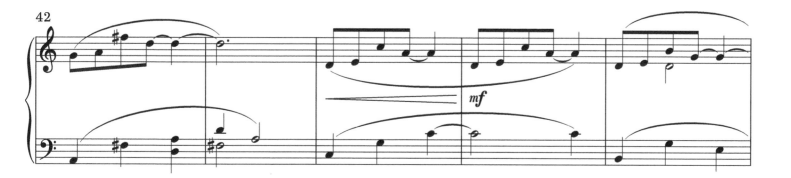

rall.   Tempo I°   rall.

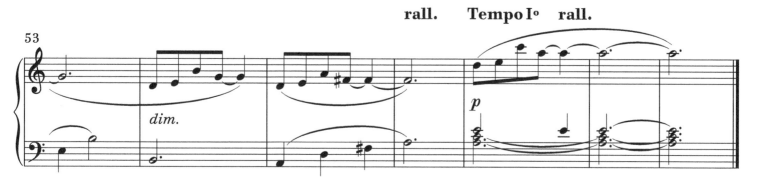

Fly Away

flight

RACHEL PORTMAN

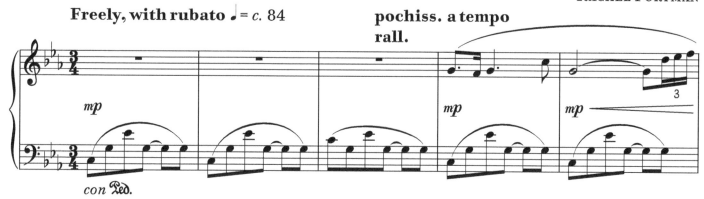

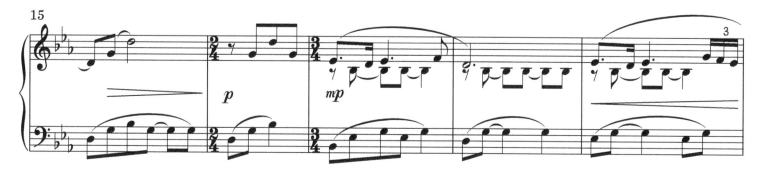

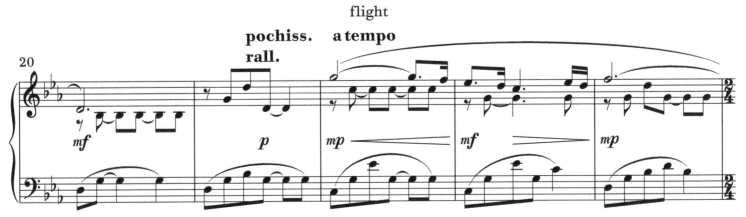

flight

pochiss. a tempo
rall.

pochiss. a tempo
rall.

rall. **a tempo**

flight

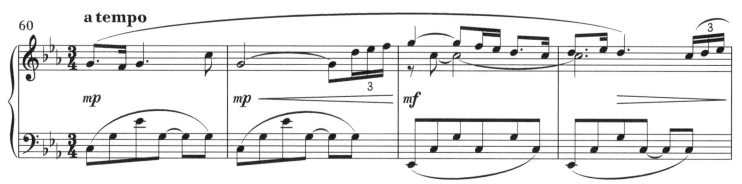

flight

flight

pochiss. rall.   a tempo

pochiss.
rall.   a tempo   pochiss. meno mosso

rall.

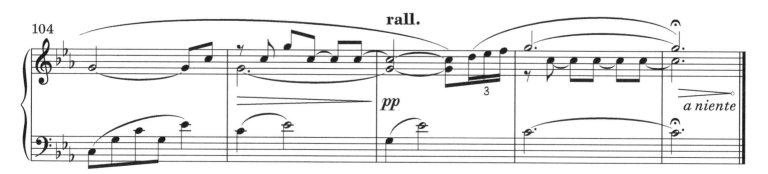

Apple Tree

Cantabile

Rachel Portman

apple tree

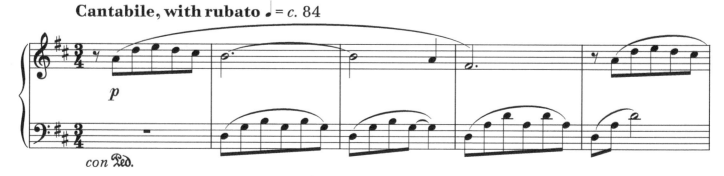

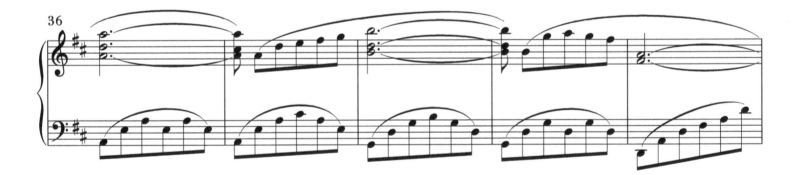

rall.   **Tempo Iº** (♩ = 84)

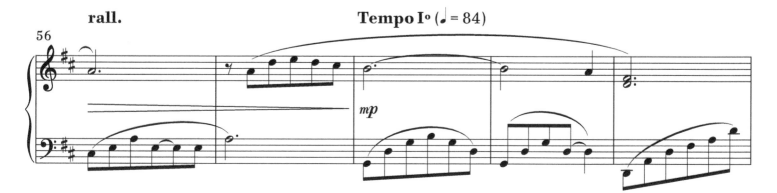

rall.

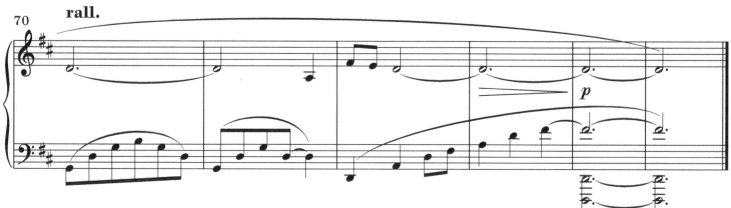

recollection

Rachel Portman

Thoughtful, tenderly with rubato ♩ = *c.* 58

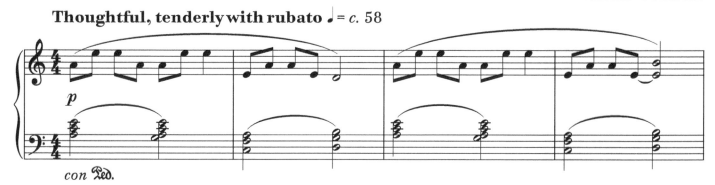

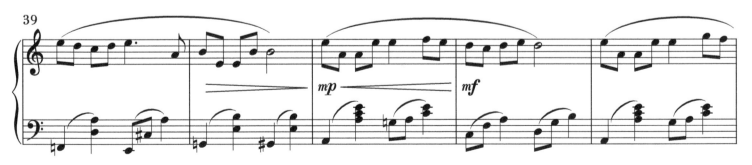

recollection

JUNIPER

juniper

Rachel Portman

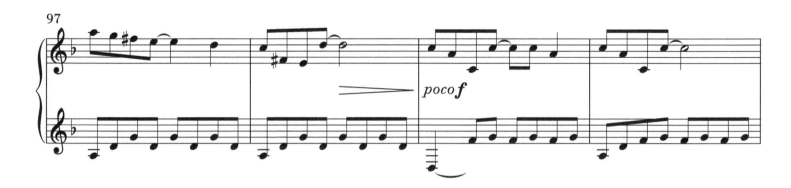

longing for spring

Rachel Portman

Gently emerging, sometimes phrases lingering
Tempo rubato ♩ = *c.* 104

con Ped.

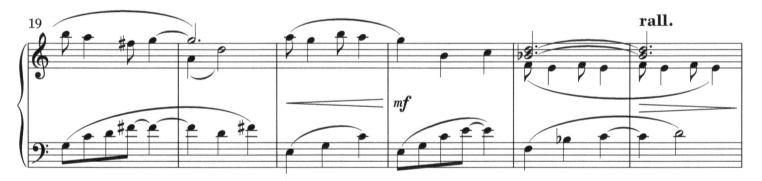

Meno mosso
(♩ = 96)

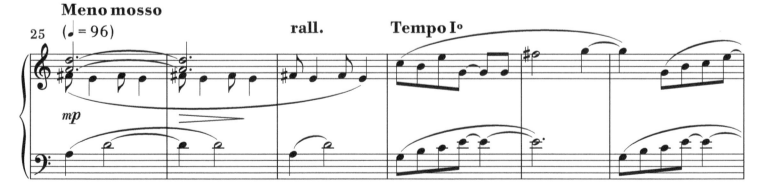

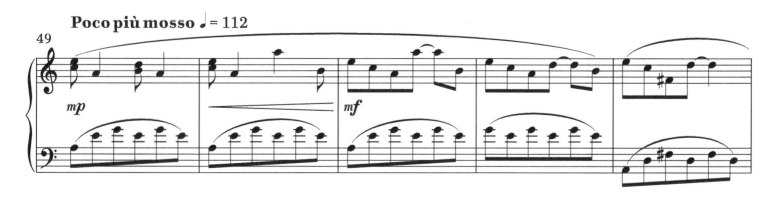

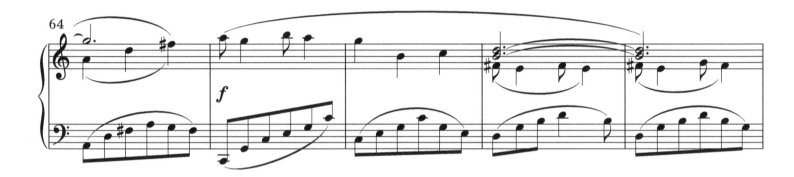

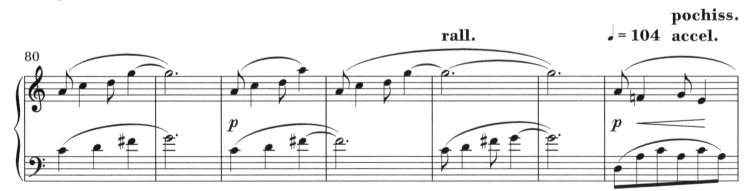

longing for spring

poco meno mosso

poco rall.

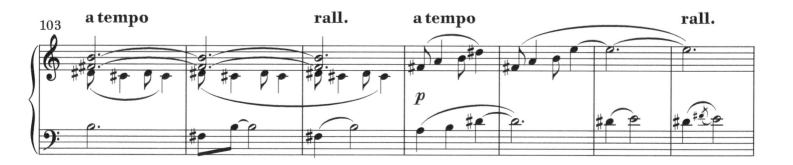

poco meno mosso

The Summer Day

the summer day

Rachel Portman

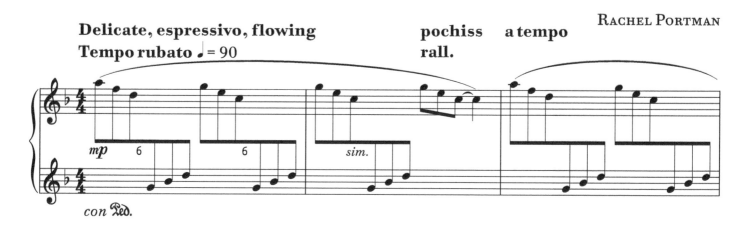

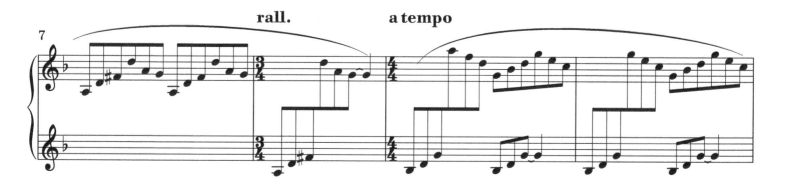

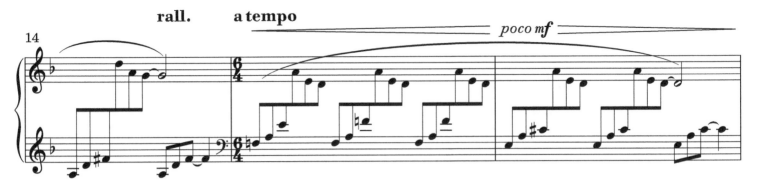

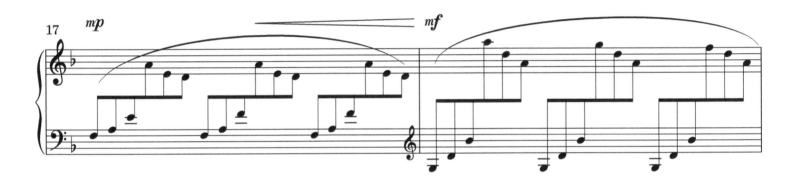

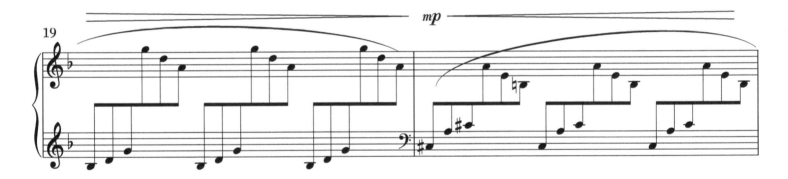

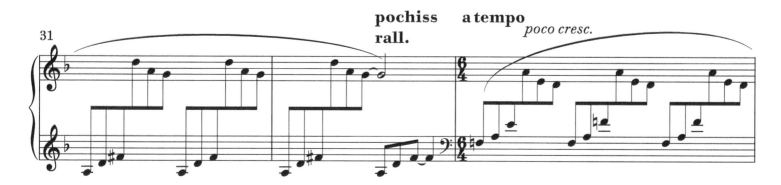

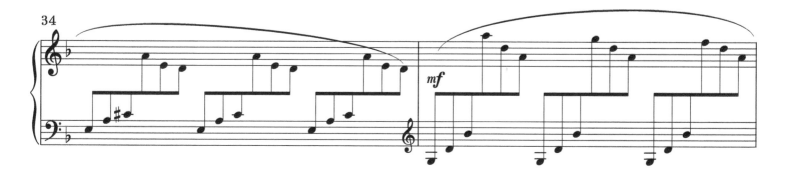

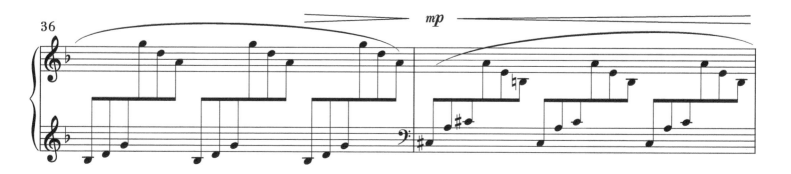

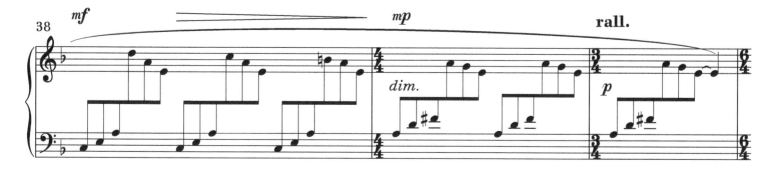

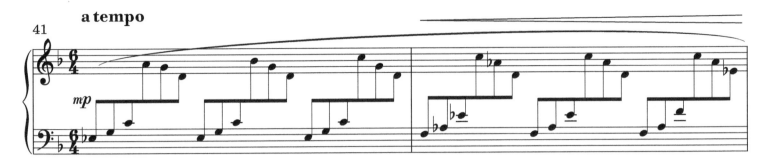

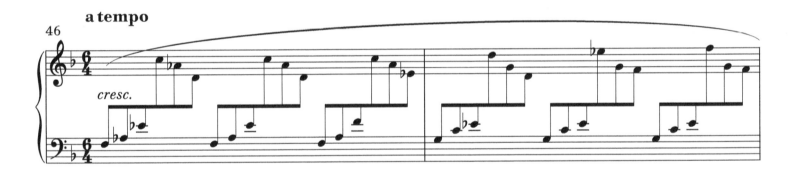

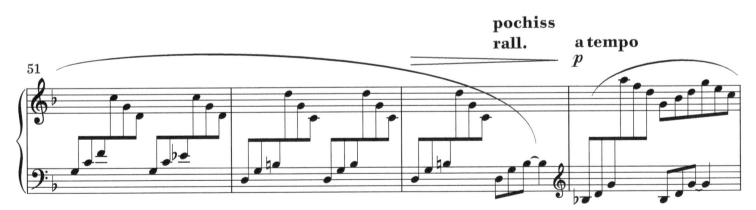

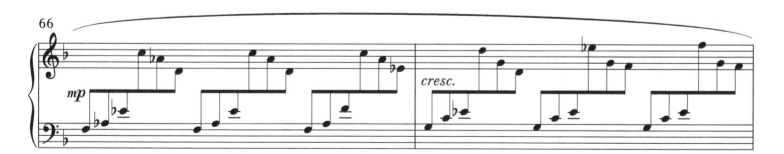

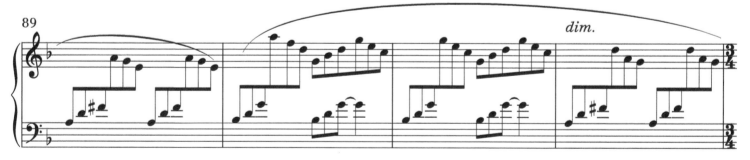

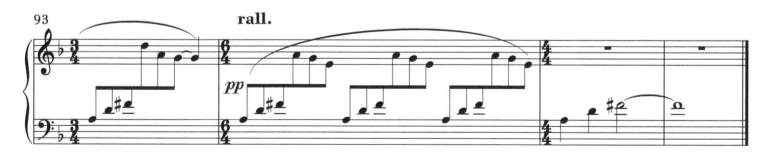

way home

Lightly, with rubato ♩ = *c.* 66

RACHEL PORTMAN

warmly, feeling of belonging

con Ped.

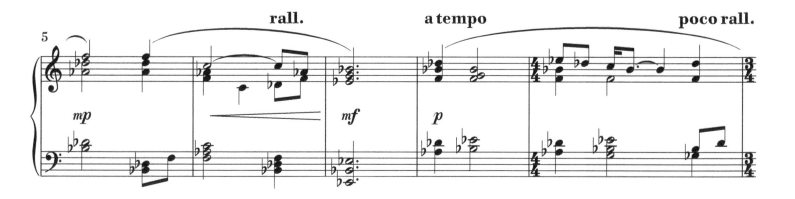

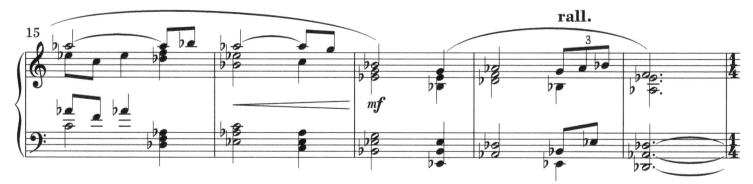

way home

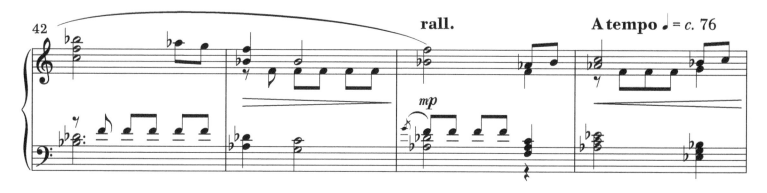

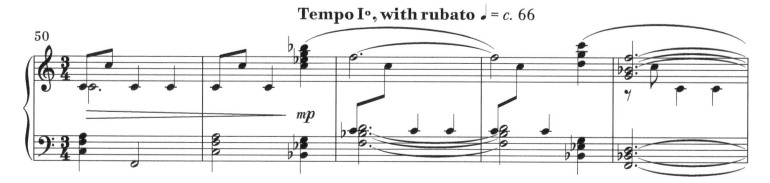

childhood

Rachel Portman

childhood